LIFE AND TIMES IN
ANCIENT EGYPT

KINGFISHER

Kingfisher Publications Plc
New Penderel House
283–288 High Holborn
London WC1V 7HZ
www.kingfisherpub.com

Based on material first published in the Sightseers series
by Kingfisher Publications Plc 1999

This edition first published by Kingfisher Publications Plc 2007
2 4 6 8 10 9 7 5 3 1

1TR/0607/TIMS/(MA)/14OMA/C

Copyright © Kingfisher Publications Plc 2007

Written and edited by: Julie Ferris, Conrad Mason, Sally Tagholm
Production controller: Aysun Ackay
DTP manager: Nicky Studdart

Illustrations by: Inklink Firenze and Kevin Maddison

A CIP catalogue record for this book
is available from the British Library.

ISBN 978 0 7534 1556 6 (paperback)
ISBN 978 0 7534 1625 9 (hardback)

Printed in China

Contents

Egyptian civilization

Thousands of years ago, a great civilization grew on the banks of the River Nile in Egypt. Under their rulers, the pharaohs, the ancient Egyptians became the most powerful nation in the Middle East. Their civilization lasted for around 3,000 years until around 31BCE, when the Romans conquered Egypt and made it part of their empire.

◁ Rameses II ruled for longer than any other pharaoh (c. 1279–1212BCE), and is often called Rameses the Great. It is said that he fathered over 100 children! This book is about Egypt's golden age under Rameses II.

Ancient Egyptian writing is among the oldest in the world. Egyptians wrote using hieroglyphs – a combination of ideograms (signs standing for ideas) and phonograms (signs standing for sound).

In 3000BCE the first pharaoh, Menes (ruled c. 3050–2950BCE), united Upper and Lower Egypt. His capital at Memphis was the largest city in the world.

The first pyramid, the Step Pyramid, was built at Saqqara by the architect Imhotep as a tomb for the Pharaoh Djoser (ruled c. 2668–2649BCE).

The great age of pyramid-building lasted for about 400 years. The largest pyramid was built at Giza for Pharaoh Khufu (ruled c. 2589–2566BCE).

▽ The Egyptian capital was at Memphis until Pharaoh Mentuhotep II reorganised the country, making Thebes the new capital. Thebes was full of temples, palaces and obelisks, and was the centre of worship for Amun, the ruler of the gods.

Egyptians' lives centred around the River Nile. The river valley and its delta were among the most lush and fertile areas in the world. This made them ideal places to build and farm.

▽ Ancient Egyptian history is divided into three different periods – the Old Kingdom, the Middle Kingdom and the New Kingdom.

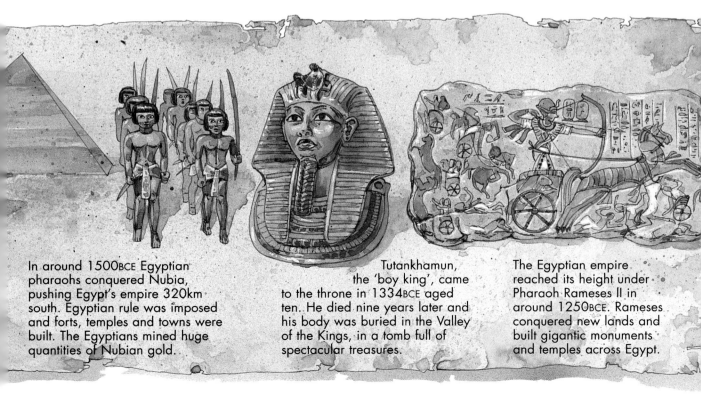

In around 1500BCE Egyptian pharaohs conquered Nubia, pushing Egypt's empire 320km south. Egyptian rule was imposed and forts, temples and towns were built. The Egyptians mined huge quantities of Nubian gold.

Tutankhamun, the 'boy king', came to the throne in 1334BCE aged ten. He died nine years later and his body was buried in the Valley of the Kings, in a tomb full of spectacular treasures.

The Egyptian empire reached its height under Pharaoh Rameses II in around 1250BCE. Rameses conquered new lands and built gigantic monuments and temples across Egypt.

Along the Nile

The River Nile was Egypt's main artery. It supplied fresh water and its fertile valley was perfect for farming and fishing. Egyptians lived close to the river, and their towns grew up along its banks. The Nile was a major transport route, bustling with small cargo boats and ships bearing vast granite columns and obelisks. It also carried funeral barges, ferrying mummies of wealthy citizens to burial.

△ Away from the river, getting around was hard work. For the pharaoh, though, riding on a palanquin (carrying chair) made it easier.

▽ Egyptians sometimes needed to travel into the desert. For this they would hire a donkey. These were cheap but very reliable animals.

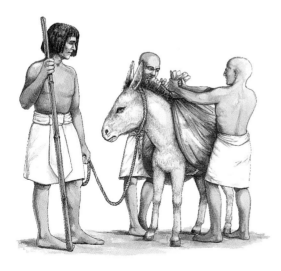

Running alongside the Nile was the 'black land', a narrow strip of inhabitable land, made fertile by water from the Nile's annual flood. Beyond this, to the east and west of the Nile, was the 'red land'. This was desert, a harsh and mysterious landscape covering more than 90 per cent of the country. Egyptians mined valuable minerals and semi-precious stones there.

▽ Great monuments were built with stone carried along the Nile. The river also helped to provide the abundant harvests that made Egypt rich.

▷ Most people lived close to the river and travelled by boat. Boats were usually made from papyrus or wood, and often had a sail.

Clothing and jewellery

Clothing in ancient Egypt was light and comfortable to keep people cool in the heat. Most clothing was made of linen. This was made from a crop called flax, grown on the banks of the Nile. Workers often wore just a loincloth, which offered little protection against the sun.

△ Wealthy Egyptians wore exquisite golden jewellery made by highly skilled craftsmen. It was often inlaid with semi-precious stones from the desert, or imported stones such as turquoise.

△ Most Egyptians went barefoot, but wealthy citizens often wore a pair of plaited papyrus sandals to protect their feet from scorpions and snakes.

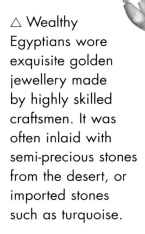

▷ Both men and women wore thick black eye paint known as kohl. This was made from ground minerals and kept in elaborate cosmetic jars like this one.

Clothing showed how important a person was. Priests dressed in white loincloths, while the pharaoh's advisors had robes. The pharaoh himself wore a crown or headdress.

When there was a banquet or a feast, rich Egyptian men and women wore braided black wigs made of human hair and held in place with beeswax. They also used perfumes made from oils and scented with myrrh and cinammon. The white linen gauze worn by the richest Egyptians was so fine that their skin could be seen beneath it.

▽ A rich Egyptian woman, dressed in fine linen and elaborate jewellery, walks past some swaying flax plants.

Food and drink

Bread and beer were the cheapest and most abundant food and drink in ancient Egypt. They were made from the wheat and barley that grew beside the river. However, there was plenty of other food available – dried fruit, vegetables, beans and fish from the river. Only the rich could afford to eat meat.

△ Egyptians drank beer using a syphon, to filter out the lumps of mashed barley.

▷ Flour was made by grinding grain between two stones. Often bits of grit got into the flour.

Women made the bread in Egypt. After grinding up wheat to make flour, they mixed in water to make dough, and poured it into a mould. Finally, they baked the dough in a clay oven. Sometimes honey or dates were added to make sweet bread.

▷ The host and the important guests at a banquet had chairs or stools. Other people used mats or cushions on the floor.

Wealthy Egyptians often held lavish banquets with dozens of courses. On the menu was duck, goose and ox, and delicacies such as gazelle, antelope and ostrich. Diners wore cones of perfumed fat on their heads. These slowly melted throughout the evening, giving off a pleasant scent.

◁ Although beer was the national drink, people also drank wine made from grapes or dates. It was stored in jars with labels, just like modern bottles.

Homes

From the pharaoh's spectacular palace to the humblest village home, all Egyptian houses were made of mud bricks. Buildings were designed to be as cool as possible, keep out thieves and resist the annual flooding.

▽ Egyptian noblemen kept splendid gardens in the countryside. They were filled with acacia and fig trees, and pools brimming with fish and lotus flowers.

△ Mud was mixed with straw and baked in the sun to make bricks. After the building was finished, the walls were whitewashed to keep the house cool. Many houses had several families living in them at once. People slept on the floor or on the roof to keep cool.

△ Most families could not afford much furniture. Beds, chairs and tables were often carved out of a local wood such as sycamore fig.

Most houses had a small yard with a clay oven for baking bread. All the cooking was done outside in case there was a fire. Near to the river, houses often had sloping walls or were built on raised platforms to keep them safe from flooding. While poor families crowded into tiny homes, the rich lived in large country villas with tiled floors and painted walls.

▽ A nobleman's estate included kitchens, cellars and stables. Most Egyptians had to bathe in the river, but nobles had their own bathrooms. They built great walls to keep out any intruders.

Markets

At the heart of an Egyptian town there was a bustling market, where people traded livestock, food and other goods. In major cities such as Memphis or Thebes, there was an amazing variety of produce on sale, both locally-grown and brought in from far away. There were pomegranates, melons and figs, sticky sweetmeats, olives, dates and over 30 different kinds of bread to choose from.

◁ Egyptian craftsmen sold beautiful vases, statues and carvings in stone, wood, metal and ivory.

▽ Large town markets were very hot and noisy, with traders bringing in their wares from far and wide. Egyptians did not use money, but used a bartering (exchange) system instead.

▽ 'Sniffer' baboons were a common sight in many markets. Like police dogs today, they were an important part of the fight against crime, helping officials track down thieves.

Egyptians traded widely with other nations. They exchanged their grain, papyrus and high-quality linen for a huge range of exotic goods, such as precious stones, gold and jewels, valuable woods, incense, spices and olive oil. Most goods were transported in boats along the Nile to markets in the larger towns.

▷ Market traders used standard weights and measures to help them work out what each item was worth in exchange. Market officials sorted out any disputes between traders.

Learning and leisure

Egyptian boys went to school, while girls stayed at home and learnt how to look after the house. In their spare time, children and adults played games. Every year there were holidays and religious festivals. The festivals included spectacular shows with acrobats, jugglers, dancers and music.

△ Egyptian children played with all sorts of different toys including dolls, model animals and spinning tops. They also played catch with balls made of clay.

▷ Egyptian schoolboys wore their hair in 'side-locks' up to the age of 12. Sometimes girls from very wealthy families were also sent to school.

▷ Boys started going to school at the age of 5 years old, and learnt how to read and write. Many hoped to get jobs as official scribes when they grew up.

▷ Only some Egyptians could afford to send their children to school. Boys from poor families started working as fishermen or farmers at a young age.

▽ Students
practised their
writing by painting
on bits of stone
or wooden slates.
They had to copy
out long stories
or lists of words.

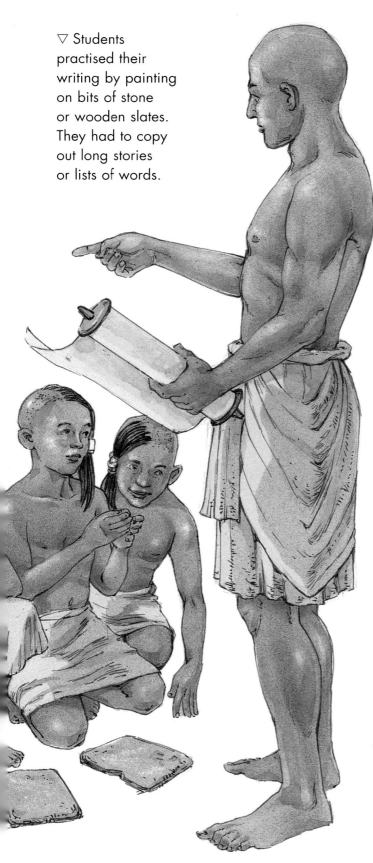

We know about some of
the pastimes Egyptians
enjoyed – partly through
paintings, and partly because
some games have survived.
Snake was a popular game,
played on a circular stone
board. Leapfrog and tug-of-
war were also favourites.

△ The Egyptians loved music. String,
wind and percussion instruments were
played at festivals and banquets. People
even sang to oxen as they threshed corn.

◁ Senet
was a very
popular board
game. It was
played with counters
and small sticks. Players
had to cross 30 squares,
overcoming obstacles to reach the
kingdom of Osiris, god of the dead.

Hunting

Hunting was the most popular pastime of all in ancient Egypt. Ordinary people hunted for fish or birds, while the pharaohs pursued big game, such as lions. Hippos were killed for their meat and because they trampled the crops.

▽ Teams of hunters in papyrus boats chased huge hippos through the water. They used lassoes to catch them and spears to weaken them.

▽ Many Egyptians hunted birds in the reed thickets of the River Nile. They travelled in small boats and hit the birds with sturdy wooden throwsticks.

▽ Cats were considered sacred in Egypt and often wore a golden ring. They were used by hunters to help catch birds and other wildlife. The Egyptian word for cat was 'Miw'.

Only noblemen hunted in the desert. They killed hares, wild bulls, gazelles, antelopes and lions. A desert hunt was a big event. Nobles rode in horse-drawn chariots and brought javelins, spears and bows and arrows, as well as hunting dogs and guides who knew the area. Sometimes they took their whole family with them as well.

19

Mummification

Egyptians believed in life after death. They preserved the dead body using a complex process called mummification, so that the person's spirit could live on forever in the afterlife.

△ As layers of linen were wrapped around a mummy, lucky amulets were bound in. They helped to make the journey to the next world as easy as possible.

▽ The body was covered with natron (a mixture of sodium and carbon) to help dry it out and preserve it before it was wrapped in linen.

▷ The brain, liver, lungs and intestines were removed from the body, dried and wrapped in linen. They were stored in canopic jars and then placed in the tomb.

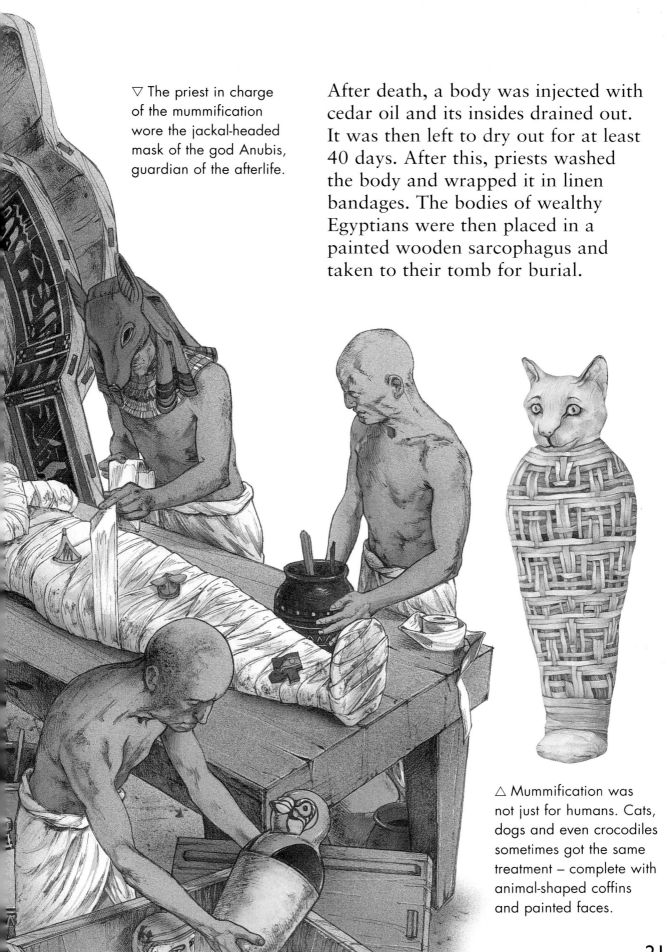

▽ The priest in charge of the mummification wore the jackal-headed mask of the god Anubis, guardian of the afterlife.

After death, a body was injected with cedar oil and its insides drained out. It was then left to dry out for at least 40 days. After this, priests washed the body and wrapped it in linen bandages. The bodies of wealthy Egyptians were then placed in a painted wooden sarcophagus and taken to their tomb for burial.

△ Mummification was not just for humans. Cats, dogs and even crocodiles sometimes got the same treatment – complete with animal-shaped coffins and painted faces.

The pyramids

The three great pyramids at Giza are among the most impressive feats of engineering that the world has ever known. They were built more than 1,200 years before the reign of Rameses II as tombs for pharaohs Khufu, Khafre and Menkure. Ordinary Egyptians had to help build the pyramids.

▷ Pharaohs were buried with their possessions for use in the afterlife. The pyramids of rich pharaohs were often targeted by tomb robbers, who would break in and steal the pharaoh's treasures.

△ The Step Pyramid at Saqqara was the first pyramid ever built in Egypt. Designed by the great architect Imhotep, it was the burial place of Pharaoh Djoser.

◁ The angles of the walls of the Bent Pyramid of Pharaoh Sneferu (ruled c. 2613–2589 BCE) at Dahshur change near the top, giving the pyramid its distinctive shape.

At 138 metres high, Khufu's pyramid was the largest stone building on earth at the time of its construction, and was one of the seven wonders of the ancient world. It is made up of more than 2.3 million limestone blocks, each one weighing at least 2.5 tonnes.

▽ The casing of polished limestone which gave the pyramids their smooth sides has now eroded away.

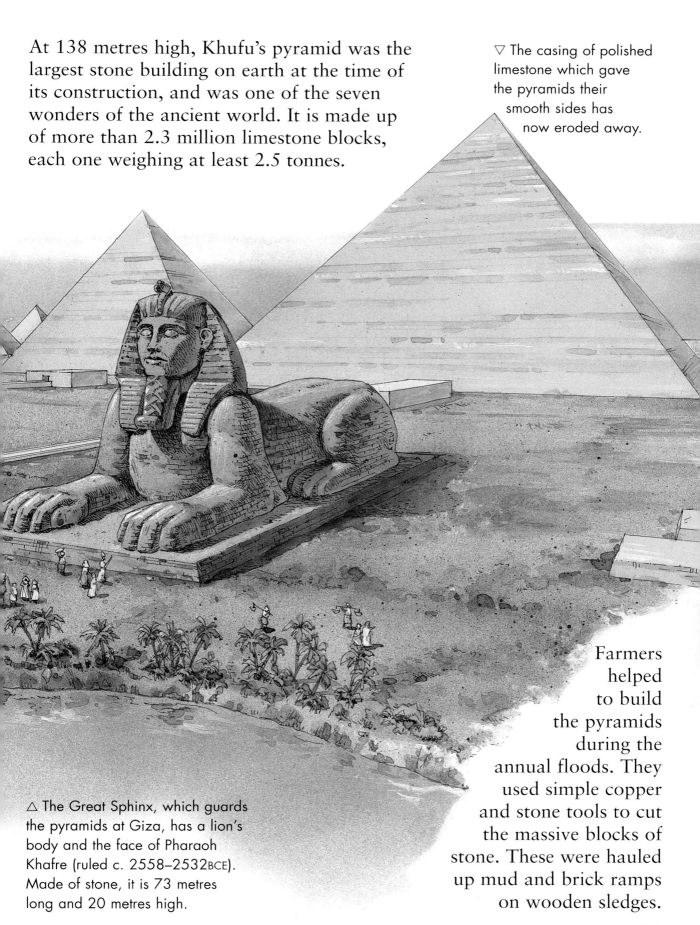

△ The Great Sphinx, which guards the pyramids at Giza, has a lion's body and the face of Pharaoh Khafre (ruled c. 2558–2532BCE). Made of stone, it is 73 metres long and 20 metres high.

Farmers helped to build the pyramids during the annual floods. They used simple copper and stone tools to cut the massive blocks of stone. These were hauled up mud and brick ramps on wooden sledges.

Karnak

In the city of Thebes stood the massive temple complex of Karnak. At the beginning, Karnak was the site of a small shrine to Amun, the king of the gods. However, it grew over the centuries to become the most important religious centre in the whole of Egypt. Each pharaoh added on more shrines and buildings, making the complex bigger and more impressive. To the Egyptians, Karnak was Ipet-isut – 'the most perfect of places'.

△ The colossal statues of Rameses II at Karnak were built to a scale unrivalled in any previous dynasties. The finishing touches were chiselled by skilled masons.

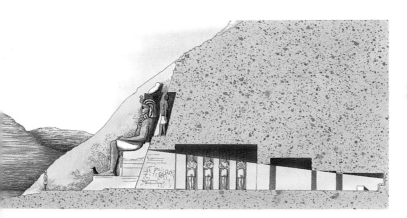

△ Overlooking the Nile at Abu Simbel, a huge temple for Pharaoh Rameses II was cut into the sandstone cliffs. It was designed so that twice a year the rays of the sun illuminated a statue of Rameses inside.

Karnak was reached by a canal running from the River Nile. Inside were living-quarters, workshops, sacred pools and storehouses. Only priests were allowed into the complex. These priests became very powerful as Karnak became richer.

The annual Opet festival was the one time of year that ordinary people had a chance to see the great statue of Amun. In this joyful festival, the statue was carried from its home, deep inside the Temple of Amun, to the temple at Luxor. The procession was a re-enactment of Amun's marriage to the goddess Mut, who had her own temple in the Karnak complex.

▽ The Hypostyle Hall in the Temple of Amun had 134 gigantic columns which were carved and painted to look like papyrus plants. When the hall flooded in the summer, it looked like a papyrus marsh.

An Egyptian farm

Most Egyptian villagers were farmers. They grew a variety of crops, fruit and vegetables on the banks of the Nile. From July to November, the river flooded the fields, leaving the soil moist and fertile for the year's farming. Crops had to be grown and harvested before the next flood.

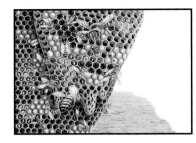

△ Honey was used as a sweetener in Egypt, and many farms had beehives.

Farming methods were simple but efficient. The most important crops were wheat, barley, flax and papyrus, but farmers also grew onions, garlic and beans, and kept cattle, sheep and pigs. Birds such as geese were reared for their eggs and meat.

▽ Farmers had animals to help them. They used oxen to plough the fields and trample the harvested grain. They even used trained monkeys to pick fruit!

▽ A shaduf was a device used to draw water from the Nile. It had a bucket on one end and a weight on the other to aid lifting.

Most of the land in Egypt was owned by the pharaoh, nobles or rich temples, but it was the ordinary people who did the hard work of planting, watering and harvesting. The success of the harvest depended on the flood. If the waters were too high, the soil was washed away. If it was too low, the crops had no water.

▷ Fishermen used small boats made of bundles of papyrus reed tied together with twine. Their fishing nets, also made of papyrus, were weighted with stones or lead.

Egyptian society

Egyptian society was arranged in a strict hierarchy. At the top was the mighty pharaoh, and at the bottom were the peasant farmers. In between were the officials, scribes and doctors who worked hard to keep the Egyptian civilization running from day to day.

The pharaoh was not only king of Egypt, but was also believed to be Horus, son of the sun god Re. As a living god he held absolute civil, religious and military power, but senior officials handled most of the day-to-day administration. The most powerful were the two viziers – one for the north and one for the south.

◁ The pharaoh sealed all official documents with his ring. This seal of Rameses II shows his name, surrounded by sacred symbols.

△ Hieroglyphs were used only on tomb and temple walls or in important matters of state. Everyday Egyptian was a much simpler language.

Justice was administered by the vizier in the great courtrooms of the capital, and by local people in the village courts. The most common punishment was a beating. For very serious crimes people were put to death.

Egyptians treated illnesses and injuries with a combination of medicine and magic. Magicians provided expert knowledge of which foods and substances could help cure which ailments. Many Egyptians also wore magical amulets to protect them from the evil spirits that were said to cause diseases. The most powerful was the eye of Horus.

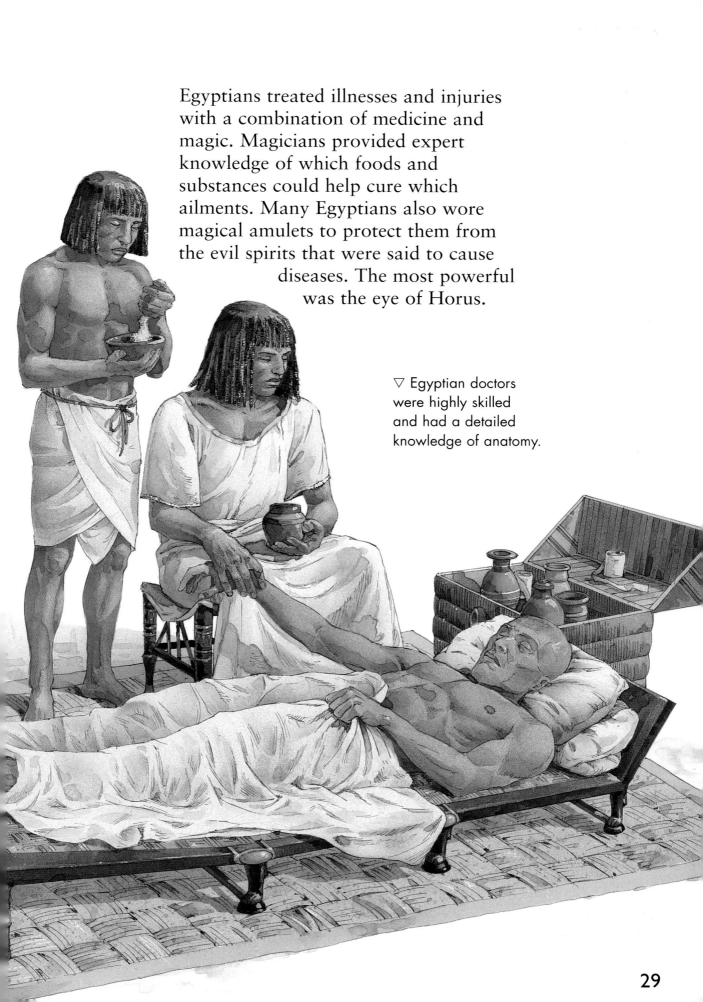

▽ Egyptian doctors were highly skilled and had a detailed knowledge of anatomy.

Quiz

Now you have learnt all about the lives of the ancient Egyptians from 1289–1224BCE, have a go at this fun quiz and test your knowledge of ancient Egypt. Answers can be found on page 32.

1. There were many different ways to get around in ancient Egypt. What was the pharaoh's favourite form of transport?

a) He rode on a small grey donkey.

b) He travelled on a large cattle vessel on the River Nile.

c) He was carried about in a palanquin, or carrying chair.

2. Ordinary Egyptian furniture, such as beds and chairs, was usually carved out of which sort of wood?

a) Ebony inlaid with gold and semi-precious stones.

b) Locally grown sycamore fig.

c) Cedar wood which was imported from Lebanon or Syria.

3. Although most Egyptians went barefoot, comfortable sandals were sometimes worn. What were they made of?

a) Locally grown fringed flax.

b) Plaited papyrus.

c) Braided human hair and beeswax.

4. During the mummification process, what was done with the brain once it had been removed from the body?

a) It was stored in a jar and later placed in the tomb.

b) It was left in the desert to be eaten by wild animals.

c) It was given to the family of the dead person.

5. To this day, the Great Sphinx stands guard over the pyramids at Giza. What does it look like?

a) It has the body of pharaoh Rameses II and the head of a ram.

b) It has the body of a crocodile and the head of pharaoh Khufu.

c) It has the body of a lion and the face of pharaoh Khafre.

6. Rameses II built the vast Hypostyle Hall in the Temple of Amun at Karnak. How did he decorate it?

a) With a sacred pool filled with lotus flowers.

b) With 65 limestone statues of the god Amun.

c) With 134 gigantic columns, carved and decorated to look like papyrus plants.

7. What kind of animal helped Egyptians in the fight against crime?

a) 'Hunter' snakes.

b) 'Sniffer' baboons.

c) 'Scout' eagles.

8. The pharaoh held absolute civil, religious and military power, but who was his second-in-command?

a) Horus, the son of Re, the sun god in human form.

b) Two chief ministers known as viziers.

c) A trained magician who had detailed knowledge of spells.

9. Egyptians enjoyed lots of different board games. How was the popular board game senet played?

a) Using counters and small sticks, players have to overcome obstacles to reach the kingdom of Osiris.

b) Using small stone balls, players must reach the centre of a circular board, coiled in the shape of a serpent.

c) Using dice and counters, a player must defeat their opponent by taking all his counters.

31

Index

Acknowledgements

Design assistance
Joanne Brown

Inklink Firenze illustrators
Simone Boni, Alessandro Rabatti, Lorenzo Pieri, Luigi Critone, Lucia Mattioli, Francisco Petracchi, Theo Caneschi.

Additional illustrations
Vanessa Card, Julian Baker, Peter Dennis, Francesca D'Ottavi, Luigi Galante, Nicki Palin, Mark Peppe, Richard Ward.

Picture credits
b = bottom, c = centre, l = left, r = right, t = top
4c The Ancient Egypt Picture Library; 7cr AKG/Erich Lessing; 8c Egyptian Museum, Cairo/AKG/Erich Lessing; 14cl Kunsthistoriches Museum, Vienna/AKG/Erich Lessing; 17cr E.T. Archive/British Museum; 19t E.T. Archive/British Library; 20bl E.T. Archive/Louvre Paris; 22bc & b The Ancient Egypt Picture Library; 28c Rockefeller Museum, Jerusalem (IDAM)/AKG/Erich Lessing; 28bl E.T. Archive/Egyptian Museum Cairo.

The publisher would like to thank the following for permission to reproduce their material. Every care has been taken to trace copyright holders. However, if there have been unintentional omissions or failure to trace copyright holders, we apologize and will, if informed, endeavour to make corrections in any future edition.

Quiz answers

1 c) 2 b) 3 b) 4 a) 5 c) 6 c) 7 b) 8 b) 9 a)